Games and After Liverpool

James Saunders

A Samuel French Acting Edition

FOUNDED 1830

SAMUELFRENCH-LONDON.CO.UK
SAMUELFRENCH.COM

FOR AMATEUR PRODUCTION ENQUIRIES

UNITED KINGDOM AND WORLD EXCLUDING NORTH AMERICA

plays@SamuelFrench-London.co.uk

020 7255 4302/01

Each title is subject to availability from Samuel French,

depending upon country of performance.

A Note on
"AFTER LIVERPOOL".

"After Liverpool" is not a play but a suite of pieces, to be
performed by one or more actors and one or more actresses.
The order in which the pieces are played is not specified. Using
a musical analogy, the script gives some themes, within and
between which any number of variations are possible.

James Saunders.

M	How do you do?
W	How do you do?
M	We haven't met. My name is.
W	How do you do?
M	How do you do? I'm a friend of.
W	My name is.
M	How do you do? I come from. I live with.
W	I was born in.
M	How interesting.
W	Not really.
M	I work at. I go to. I drive past. I walk up.
W	That must be a bore.
M	Not really. I get up. I run over. I fly past. I come across. I knock back. All grist to the mill.
W	I put over. I take from. I take out, I take out, I take out.
M	Tiresome.
W	Not really.
M	I put on. I put off, I hang up, I run down, I take, from, I. I saw you across the room. I wanted to meet you.
W	Well, here we are.
M	And now we know each other.
W	Not really.
M	Not really.

| M | Favourite colour. |
| | |

M   Favourite colour.

[M   Red.
W   Blue.

M   Favourite flower.

[M   Rose.
W   Tulip.

M   Favourite sport.

[M   Football.
W   Tennis.

M   Favourite food.

[M   Fish.
W   Steak.

W   I like my steak.

[M   Medium rare.
W   Rare.

M   Favourite wine.

[M   White.
W   Red.

W   Favourite holiday place.

[M   Normandy.
W   Brittany.

[M   Scissors.
W   Stone.

M   Do you like Brahms?

She shakes her head

M   What about student power then?

W   You mean sit-ins and so forth?

M   Well yes, for instance, what about student sit-ins?

W   But of course one can't consider these things in isolation.

M   No no, that goes without saying. But you think they have a case?

W   Don't you think they have a case?

M	I suppose everybody has a case if you think about it.
W	I suppose they do.
M	Has a case or is a case.
W	Hm?
M	If they don't have a case they must be a case.
W	The students?
M	Well, anyone.
W	That's true.
M	Black power, white power, student power.
W	Tyrone Power.
M	No, I'm serious.
W	I'm sorry.
M	It's all right. I'm sorry.
W	I'm sorry.
M	What about the students then?
W	Fuck the students.
M	Hm?
W	Yes, I think they have a case, after all if one looks at the situation in perspective it is a bit of an anomoly in this day and age, after all, it is a third of one's life one's considering, a third of one's life from the age of five till at least the teens, imposed upon one, by law or economic necessity, after all, one should have some say, obviously, after all . . .
M	Listen. I want.
W	Hm?
M	Do go on.

M	Was I good?
W	What do you mean by good?
M	Did you enjoy it?
W	I always enjoy it.
M	Yes, but.
W	Yes but what?

M	You always enjoy it?
W	Yes, I think so.
M	With anyone?
W	I don't do it with anyone.
M	With anyone you do it with.
W	One way or another, yes.
M	You always enjoy it the same.
W	Of course not the same.
M	I mean equally.
W	No, no, some times are better than others.
M	Some people.
W	Some people at some times are better than other people at other times.
M	Well?
W	What is it you want to know?
M	You don't give much away, do you?
W	What do you want me to say?
M	Did you enjoy it . . . ?
W	I told you, yes.
M	I haven't finished.
W	I'm sorry. Go on. Did I enjoy it.
M	Did you enjoy it — more. . . .
W	Than what?
M	Than before.
W	I haven't done it with you before.
M	With the others.
W	Did I enjoy it with you more than I enjoyed it with the others.
M	If you like.
W	Not if I like. It's your question.
M	All right then.
W	So that's the question you want answered. Did I enjoy it more with you than I enjoyed it with the others.
M	Look, if you don't want to answer.
W	Who said I don't want to answer.
M	Then why don't you?
W	I'm trying to. But I have to know the question.

M	Well now you know it. I don't see that it's such an unreasonable question.
W	I didn't say it was.
M	Well?
W	More than *any* of the others?
M	More than —! I ask a simple question. . . .
W	I'm asking a simple question. Do you mean did I enjoy it with you more than I enjoyed it with any one of the others?
M	Oh, let's forget it.
W	Why?
M	You obviously don't propose to answer it.
W	I do propose to answer it. I just want to get the question straight. You're the one who won't answer *my* question.
M	What question?
W	Do you mean more than *any* of the others?
M	How many were there anyway?
W	There you are, you won't answer. How can I answer you if you won't answer me?
M	You're not answering *me*, are you?
W	I asked first.
M	*I* asked first. A simple question. . . .
W	Of which you don't want the answer.
M	Then why did I ask?
W	All right, I'll tell you. I didn't enjoy it very much.
M	With me.
W	Mm, I didn't enjoy it much with you. I enjoyed it, but not much. Neither did you, did you?
M	No. You were too stiff.
W	You weren't stiff enough.
M	So now we know.
W	We knew all along.

M   Do you love me?
W   Why do you ask?
M   Why don't you answer?
W   Why do you want to know?
M   Why do you never answer my questions?
W   Why are you always asking questions? Why do you have to verbalise everything?
M   Why do you never say what you feel? Why do we always quarrel?
W   I love you. Do you love me?

W   One of the things I like about being with you is that I don't feel obliged to talk all the time. It's easy to be silent with you. Being silent with you, close but not touching, eyes closed, not communicating with any of the five senses, just knowing you're there, feeling you're there, something else takes over, difficult to put into words because words belong to the five senses and this is something else. Something other. An awareness. It's hard to describe it. A feeling that you are somewhere inside me, I am somewhere inside you. Outside the senses, beyond time and space, outside ourselves. I can't put it into words. But it's there. Do you feel that?
M   Hm?
W   Do you feel that.
M   I'm sorry, I wasn't listening.

W   Listen. I want to ask you something.
M   Go on.
W   Do you see me merely as a sexual object?
M   Is this serious?
W   Yes.

M   I object to merely for a start.

W   Do you see me only as a sexual object.

M   I haven't thought about it.

W   Then think about it.

M   Why do you ask?

W   I just wondered.

M   Why? What have I done?

W   Never mind.

M   Hm?

W   Forget it.

M   What's the matter?

W   Oh, it's hopeless.

M   What's hopeless?

W   We never answer each other's questions. Have you noticed? We just add more questions.

M   I suppose you mean I do.

W   We both do. We put up great barriers of questions that never get answered. We cover ourselves with questions we don't want answered. It's not communication, it's — ping-pong.

M   I thought we were getting along all right.

W   We are not getting along all right. In bed we are getting along all right.

M   That's something.

W   Yes, that's something.

M   You think we don't communicate?
       That's a question.

W   No. We don't communicate. We do not communicate.

M   News to me.

W   It's not news to you.

M   When did we stop communicating?

W   We never started.

M   Oh.

W   Oh.

M   So what do you. . . .
       So what do you propose we should do about it?

W   Go to bed?

M   No.

W   Really?

M   You're very bitter suddenly.

W   Am I?

M   You know you are.
         Why?

W   I don't know.

M   And why do you want to pass it on to me?

W   I don't know.
         No, don't touch me. That's the easy solution.

M   I didn't mean it as a solution.

W   Didn't you? To cut a disagreeable conversation short?
         Because words won't do it?

M   I'm not sure, quite, what's worrying you.

W   That's what's worrying me.

M   Look. . . .

W   Don't touch me. Please.
         It's not quite true that we never communicated. We used
         to communicate. Desire, and desirability, that's what
         we trafficked in. I find you desirable, do you find me
         desirable, I want you, do you want me.

M   Used to?

W   We don't need to any more, do we? It's understood.
         The desire comes easy, the bed comes easy, the language
         has lost its purpose, who needs it? We're left with a
         game we play between fucks.
         I want us to use language together —as we use our bodies
         together. Is that unreasonable?
         Come on . . . Let's go to bed.

W   Do you love me?

M   Yes. Do you love me?

W   Yes. Do you love me?

M   Yes. Do you love me?

W   Yes. Do you love me?

M	Yes. Do you love me?
W	Then why do we keep asking?

W	Do you want an apple?
M	Yes, please.
W	Here you are.
M	Is that the only one?
W	Yes. Go on, have it.
M	No no. I wouldn't dream of it.
W	Go on.
M	What about you?
W	Don't worry about me.
M	Don't you want one?
W	Look, I'm offering it to you, aren't I?
M	I don't want it if you want it.
W	I thought you said you did want it.
M	Not if you want it. Not the last one.
W	The last one tastes the same as all the others. Whether I want it or not.
M	Of course it doesn't. Look, do you really expect me to sit here eating the last apple knowing you might like it yourself? Do you? Honestly, you have such a low opinion of me.

W	Do you want an apple?
M	Are you having one?
W	Do you want an apple?
M	I'll have one if you do.
W	Why if I do? Do you want one or not?
M	All right, let's both have an apple.

W   There's only one apple.
M   Only one? You have it.
W   But I don't want it.
M   I wish you wouldn't bother me with your problems.

M   Are there any apples?
W   Yes, there's one left.
M   Only one?
W   Yes.
M   I'll leave it then.
W   Have it.
M   No, I won't take the last one.
W   Why not?
M   Someone might want it.
W   But you want it.
M   Not really.

W   There's one apple left.
M   Oh?
W   You'd better have it.
M   Why me?
W   I don't want you feeling aggrieved because I've taken
       the last apple.
M   Don't be ridiculous. If you want it, have it. If you don't,
       leave it where it is.
W   All right.
M   You're really going to eat it are you? The last bloody
       apple.

W	I'd love an apple, wouldn't you?
M	Mm.
W	Oh, there's only one left.
M	You have it, darling.
W	No, you have it, darling.
M	No you have it darling.
W	No you have it darling.
M	No you have it darling.
W	No you have it. Darling.

W	Here is an apple. See the apple. I want the apple. Do you want the apple?
M	I want the apple. I also want you to have the apple.
W	I also want you to have the apple. Shall we split the apple?
M	But if we split the apple, we shall have nothing to argue about.

W	Hey.
M	Hm?
W	Catch.
M	Thanks.
W	Eat.
M	Catch.
W	Thanks.
M	Eat.
W	Catch...

W	So you're going at last.
M	Seems like it.
W	Is that yes or no?
M	Unless you've got some other idea.
W	I've run out of ideas. Why, do you have any other ideas?
M	If I had I suppose I wouldn't be going, would I?
W	I suppose not. Anyway, I've tried everything.
M	*You've* tried everything?
W	We've both tried everything, I suppose. I suppose there's no point in hanging on. No point in trying again. No point in going over the same old ground again and again and again. Best to give up, I suppose. Cut one's losses. Go, go. Try with somebody else.
M	There's nobody else.
W	You'll find somebody else.
M	So will you.
W	I daresay. Not to worry about me.
M	We did agree it would be best.
W	I know we agreed. I'm saying, go, go. Only.
M	Only what?
W	It's your decision.
M	My decision!
W	Just so long as you realise. It's your decision.
M	We both agreed. . . .
W	We both agreed but it's your decision, it's still your decision. You're the one who's going.
M	One of us has to go.
W	And you're the one. You've made the decision to go. I haven't. I can't make decisions for you. Just so long as you realise.
M	Do you want me to go or not?
W	I want you to make your own decision and do your own thing. I'm not going to hold you back. If you want to go. I also don't want to be —held responsible —if you do.
M	Do you want me to go?
W	I want you to do as you think fit!

M   Do you want me to go!
         Do you want me to go!!
W   No.
         Do you want to go?
M   No.
         Oh, what else is there to say?
W   We'll find something.

W   Let's play a game.
M   What kind of a game?
W   Question and answer. If you answer with a question you
         lose.
M   Go on then.
W   Do you love me?
M   I don't know what love is.
W   You lose.
M   It wasn't a question.
W   It wasn't an answer.
M   But if I don't know what you're talking about. . . .
W   If you don't know what I'm talking about the answer's
         no. You lose. Your turn.
M   When did you stop beating your husband?
W   Foul. I'm not having i . Again.
M   Erm. . . .
W   Come on. Not a single question you want answered?
M   All right. Do you love *me*
W   Yes.
M   Do you love me. . . .
W   My turn.
M   Do you love me whatever I do?
W   What on earth do you mean?
M   You lose.
W   No. . . .
M   You don't?

W   I mean no, it's an unfair question.

M   Why?

W   Well, because. . . . Well, all right, yes, I suppose if I love you I must still love you whatever you do. I mean — somewhere deep inside I must still love you whatever you do. I mean — somewhere deep inside I must still love you whatever you do — within reason. I suppose.

M   Hedging it in a bit, aren't you?

W   I told you, it's an unfair question.

M   Why?

W   Because. . . . Yes, because "whatever you do" implies limitless possibilities and I don't love a creature of limitless possibilities, I love you, and you are defined, the you I love, by your limits, your character, your behaviour within limits.

M   Very clever.

W   It's not clever, it's fact.

M   And whose are the limits? Mine or yours?

W   Yours. I don't want to limit the person I love.

M   But surely whatever I do, I do, and therefore it's within my limits. If I *do* it. *I* do it.

W   Well — yes, all right.

M   So speaking practically, you love me — whatever I do.

W   Have you got something on your mind?

M   Do you?

W   Well — yes, all right, yes. I love you whatever — whatever you do. Within. . . .

M   Within my limits.

W   Yes. Yes. I mean you're not the sort of man to commit, say a gratuitous act of cruelty. So it doesn't apply. Loving you, I can understand the — necessity for what you do, and therefore still love you. In — in spite of it. I mean in spite of perhaps not liking whatever it is you're — going to do. . . .

M   Do you love me?

W   *Yes.*

M   Do you love me?

W   Yes.

M   Do you love me?
                He hits her
W   So that's it. Yes, yes. . . .
M   Do you love me?
                He hits her
W   Yes. You've made your point. Yes.
                He hits her
         Stop it.
                He hits her
M   Do you love me?
W   I tell you yes, now stop it.
                He hits her
         It's not funny.
                He hits her
M   Do you love me?
W   You're hurting. Yes.
                He hits her
M   Yes?
W   Yes.
                He hits her
         Yes.
                He hits her
         Yes. Yes!! Yes, you bastard, yes!!

The MAN is talking
W   Just a minute, can you stop?
M   What's the matter?
W   I'm bored with this conversation.
M   You're what?
W   The conversation doesn't interest me.
M   Oh?
W   Can you talk about something else?

M   Certainly, if you want me to. I do apologise for boring you.

W   Not you, your conversation. You weren't to know, I
     was trying to look interested. My fault.

M   You mean you should have looked bored?

W   No, I should have told you straight away I wasn't
     interested.

M   Hm. Does this often happen?

W   What?

M   Finding yourself saddled with a crashing bore?

W   You are not a crashing bore.

M   Just an ordinary bore.

W   I've offended you.

M   Me? Why should I be offended. You're the one who
     should be offended, having to put up with a crashing
     bore.

W   You are not. . . .

M   After all, if one's a crashing bore it's best that one's told.
     Thank you. For telling me. That I'm a. . . .

W   Stop it.

M   Am I boring you again?

W   Listen. Stop it and listen, be quiet and shut up and
     listen. It's quite simple. You were talking about
     something which didn't interest me. I should have let
     you know at once. Instead I pretended to be interested.
     It was my mistake. I apologise.

M   Oh, don't apologise, I should apologise, I'm the bore.

W   You're not *listening*. . . .

M   And now I have news for you. May I tell it, at the risk
     of boring you?

W   Go on.

M   This conversation is boring *me*. So shall we change the
     subject? Or better still, since we both find each other
     such crashing bores, perhaps I'll put the television on.

W   I don't want television, I want to talk to you.

M   In spite of the fact that I'm. . . .

W   Please. Stop it, please, please.

M   The sad thing is, I was only telling you that story
           because I thought you might be interested. It was of no
           interest to me.

M   How would you like to go to the cinema tonight?
W   Tonight?
M   If you're not doing anything else.
W   No, I'm not doing anything else.
M   How about it then?
W   Erm. Yes, all right. If you like.
M   Not if I like. If you like. Do you want to go?
W   You want to go, don't you?
M   If you do.
W   Mm. All right, then.
M   You don't sound terribly enthusiastic. Is there anything
           else you want to do.
W   No no.
M   Or we could stay in. We don't have to go out.
W   We may as well. No reason why not.
M   The reason why not would be if you didn't want to go.
W   I've told you, I'll come if you're going.
M   I don't want to drag you out just because you think I
           want to go.
W   Don't you want to go then?
M   I want to go if you want to go. Do you want to go to
           the cinema or not?
W   Yes. Erm. Yes, yes.
M   You're sure?
W   I'm sure, yes.
M   You don't sound very sure.
W   I'm easy. If you're going I'll come with you.
M   Just because I'm going?
W   I don't care either way, honestly. I'll stay in or I'll go
           out. I honestly don't give a damn either way.

M   Oh, well, let's stay in, for God's sake.

W   Why?

M   There's no point going if you don't want to go.

W   There is a point. *You* want to go.

M   I don't want to go to the bloody cinema. I just thought
       you might like to go to the cinema. I do wish you'd say
       what you want now and then.

W   So. We're in for another jolly evening at home, are we?

_____

M   Well, and what's a pretty girl like you doing in a place
       like this?

W   Oh, sir, she said.

M   Do you come here often.

W   That's a leading question.

M   I meant it to be. You know what they say.

W   Make hay while the sun?

M   I was thinking of "When opportunity knocks".

W   The wolf is at the door.

M   Oh come, now, my intentions are strictly dishonourable.

W   Famous last words.

M   But seriously.

W   Oh, if you're going to be serious.

M   Never fear, I'm not the type.

W   That's what they all say.

M   Do I look it?

W   I never judge by appearances.

M   Is that what your mother taught you?

W   Together with "Beware of dark strangers".

M   You must be missing a lot of fun.

W   That would be telling.

M   Mind you, I realise you're probably overwhelmed by
       my animal magnetism.

W   My word he fancies himself.

M   You, actually.

W   There's nothing like coming straight to the point.

M   I don't believe in beating about the bush.

W   The masterful type.

M   Any objections?

W   Actually I rather like it.

M   Well isn't that lucky?

W   There is a divinity, you see.

M   So what shall we do now?

W   Ah, now, I have a golden rule.

M   Do tell.

W   Always let the gentleman lead.

M   Beautiful *and* intelligent.

W   Thank you, mein Herr.

M   My move then.

W   Exactly. You were saying?

M   Now now, you mustn't appear too eager, it's not becoming.

W   Haven't you noticed? We're emancipated. You were saying.

M   Oh, well, in that case, I say, do you want to stay here?

W   I can think of better things to do.

M   Such as?

W   Well, have you any suggestions?

M   I have actually.

W   I wonder if it's what I'm thinking?

M   I wonder. Let's leave and find out, shall we?

W   What a very good idea.

M   Erm. . . .

W   Something on your mind?

M   Well, you know, as I said I don't like beating about the bush. I like to get things straight. To avoid misunderstandings.

W   Very commendable. What would my lord and master like to know?

M   Do you fuck?
                 She hits him. Or:
W   How dare you.

M   What's wrong?
W   Hm?
M   What's the matter?
W   With what?
M   With you.
W   Nothing as far as I know. Why?
M   Something obviously is.
W   Why, what have I said?
M   You haven't said anything.
W   Well then.
M   You still manage to make it pretty obvious you're upset
         about something.
W   I don't know what gives you that idea. You're probably
         feeling a bit morose, so you imagine I'm upset.
M   I'm not morose.
W   No? You're not exactly cheerful, are you?
M   Do you expect me to be cheerful when you're like this?
W   Like what?
M   You know very well.
W   Are you blaming me for it?
M   For what?
W   For your moroseness.
M   I'm not morose and I'm not blaming you for anything.
W   Oh do leave me alone.
         I don't know why it is you take everything so personally.
M   What are you talking about?
W   The minute I'm a little under the weather you go around
         as if it's the end of the world. You make me feel so
         guilty.
M   If you'd just tell me what I've done wrong.

W   Why shouldn't I feel a bit low now and then? You're
        depressed often enough. I don't automatically assume
        it's something I've done.
M   I know you don't.
W   You mean it usually is something I've done.
        Oh do leave me alone.
        If I'm such a depressing influence why don't you go out?
M   I don't want to go out and leave you like this.
W   You're not doing much good staying in, are you? Face
        as long as a fiddle.
        You're only making me feel guilty.
M   Look, I can't help it if I'm affected by your moods.
W   Moods. Is that what you think they are?
M   I can't be happy if you're upset. I'm sorry. . . .
W   Well I'm very sorry but there's nothing I can do about it.
M   I'm not saying there is.
W   Well then. Go out, leave me alone. Go out and have a
        drink or something. I'll be all right. No point in both of
        us being miserable.
M   Oh God. . . .
        I'm no help, am I?
W   Obviously not.
M   Well am I? Is there anything I can do?
W   No. I said no.
M   I'm going out then.
W   Where to?
M   I don't know. For a walk.
        All right?
W   Wait.
M   What?
W   Don't leave me.

W   Face.
M   Eyes.
W   Sea.

M	Shell.
W	Sand.
M	Beach.
W	Nuts.
M	Crazy.
W	Love.
M	Apple.
W	Pip.
M	Lieutenant.
W	Lieutenant?
M	Lieutenant.
W	Right tenant.
M	House.
W	Flat.
M	Horizontal.
W	Love.
M	Tennis.
W	Racquet.
M	Din.
W	Din-din.
M	Baby.
W	Love.
M	Like.
W	Love.
M	Like!
W	Peas.
M	Peas?
W	Like as two peas.
M	Twins.
W	Gemini.
M	Aquarius.
W	Hair.
M	Pubic.
W	Love.
M	Philtre.
W	Percolator.

M   Coffee.
W   Pot.
M   Kettle.
W   Black.
M   Sin.
W   Love.
M   Dove.
W   Peace.
M   Quiet.
W   Silent.
M   Night.
W   Love.
M   Bed.
W   Love.
M   Bed.
W   Love.
M   Hate.
W   No.
M   Go on.
W   No.
M   Hate.
       Go on. Hate.
W   Erm.
       Erm.
M   Go on. Hate. Hate hate hate.
W   Erm.

W   Talk to me.
M   Hm?
W   Talk to me.
M   What do you want me to say?
W   I don't know.
M   Well then.
W   Just talk.

M   I haven't any news.
W   I don't want news.
M   Then what do you want?
W   I don't know. Communication, I suppose.
M   Communication? What on earth do you mean by
        communication?
W   I don't know.
M   I'm not fond of talking for the sake of talking, you
        should know that.
W   I don't want you to talk for the sake of talking.
M   Then what do you want?
W   I don't know.
M   I've nothing to say. Do you have something to say?
W   No. . . .
M   Then how can we talk if we've nothing to say?
W   I don't know.
        It's a comforting noise, I suppose.
M   A comforting noise?
W   Yes. A comforting noise.
M   Hm.
W   At least it allows us to.
M   Allows us to what?
W   Allows us to pretend we're communicating at least.
M   Why should we pretend to communicate if we've
        nothing to communicate? I don't see the point in it. Do
        you?
W   I suppose not.
M   Well, we're talking. And all you can say is you don't
        know and you suppose not. What a meaningless
        conversation.
W   Yes. Meaningless. So we have nothing to say to each
        other.
M   Why should we have anything to say to each other?
W   I don't know.
M   You don't know.
W   No. I don't know. I simply find it rather strange.
M   What do you find rather strange?

W   I find it rather strange that after so long, we have
nothing to say to each other. Nothing to communicate.

M   Why do you find it strange?

W   You don't find it strange then?

M   I'd have thought it obvious that after so long we'd have
nothing to say to each other.

W   Why do you think it obvious?

M   Because we've said it. Because it has already been said.
Because we know each other. We've nothing to
communicate because we know each other.

W   This stops communication?

M   If we know each other what is there left to
communicate?

W   I don't know.

M   You don't know.

W   No. I don't know. So. So, you think we know each
other.

M   I should think after so long we should know each other.
Don't you think we know each other?
Don't you think we know each other?
What is it you want? What's the matter?
What are you trying to say?

W   I'm not sure I know what it is, to know someone. I
don't think I understand what it is.

M   How can you not know what it is? You've known
people, haven't you? You know me. That's what it is.

W   I don't think so.

M   What do you mean, you don't think so?

W   You least of all.

M   What a stupid conversation this is.

W   No, I don't know you. Whatever it is, to know
somebody, I don't know you. You are a stranger to me.
A complete stranger.

M   After so long I'm a stranger?

W   Yes, after so long. And the longer it gets, the more of a
stranger you are. That's odd, isn't it? I remember when
we first knew each other, I mean when we first met, I
was beginning to, I think, know you slightly. Then

	something happened. Do you know, now, I think you are more of a stranger than when I first met you?
M	I find that hard to believe.
W	I find it hard to believe.
M	And why is it, do you think? That I'm a stranger to you? Or don't you know? Well, I'm sorry you don't know me, or no longer know me, perhaps I've changed out of all recognition.
W	I don't think so.
M	If you used to know me and no longer do, I should think I must have changed? Mustn't I?
W	Or I've forgotten.
M	Or, of course, you've forgotten. I hadn't thought of that. I had no idea your memory was so bad. Oh, this is a stupid conversation, is this what you wanted? This kind of ridiculous conversation?
M	Well, at least I know you. So we are not completely cut off from each other.
W	What you mean is, you know my habits. You know my likes and dislikes. You know how much sugar I have in my tea.
M	Oh, come now.
W	How much sugar I have in my tea. That's what it comes to. Plus which of my habits irritate you, and which of my habits don't.
M	You may be right about you. You are not right about me.
W	The rest we've forgotten. If we ever knew anything else.
M	Well, well.
W	You don't believe me.
M	Am I supposed to be taking this conversation seriously?
W	I don't think it matters.
M	No. tell me. Am I? If you wish, I shall. Is that why you wanted me to talk to you? So that we could discuss the strange fact that all we know of each other after all these years is how much sugar we have in our tea? Or is the conversation, this meaningless conversation, supposed to have some therapeutic effect?
W	Therapeutic effect?

M	Shall we know each other better afterwards, do you think?
W	I shouldn't think so.
M	No?
W	Why should we?
M	Pity. So the conversation really is meaningless, is it?
W	Yes, I think so.
M	Delightful.
W	Because, of course, as you must know, what you call "this conversation" is nothing of the kind.
M	Oh? What is it, then, if it isn't a conversation?
W	A conversation is people talking to each other. We are not talking to each other.
M	Oh, are we not? My mistake, I assumed we were. What are we doing, then?
W	We are talking to ourselves. We are talking to ourselves.

M	Hallo. Hallo.
W	Hallo.
M	Is anyone there?
W	Is anyone there? Hallo.
M	Who is that, please?
W	Who's speaking?
M	Hallo.
W	Who's speaking?
M	I can't hear you. Hallo.
W	Would you speak up?
M	I can't hear you. Who's speaking?
W	Who is it?
M	Hallo.
W	Who is it?
M	I can't hear you.

W   Who's speaking I can't hear you, would you speak up.

Pause

Hallo.
Hallo.

Pause

Hallo.
Hallo.

M   Hallo.

W   Hallo, we were cut off.

M   Are you there?

W   We were cut off, is that you? I can't hear you very well.

M   The line's bad, I can't hear. Is it you? Who is it, is it you?

W   Can't you speak up? I can't hear you, I can't hear what you're saying.

M   Can you speak up.

W   Who is that? Is it you? Will you please speak louder.

M   I can't hear you.

Pause

Hallo.

Pause

Hallo.

W   (immediately) Hallo.

{M
{W   Hallo.

{M   It is you, is it?
{W   Can you hear me?

{M   The line is very bad, you are there, are you?
{W   Can you speak more clearly, I think there's something wrong with the line.

{M   I'm sorry, I can't understand you, can you speak louder!
{W   There's too much noise, I can't hear who you are!

{M   Will you please . . . !
{W   Can you please . . . !

M   Hallo.

Pause

W   Hallo.

Pause

M   Hallo.

         Pause

    Hallo.

         Silence

W   I'm sorry.
Forgive me?
I really am.
Are you *very* upset?
What can I do to make up?
You are, aren't you? I've hurt you. Haven't I?
What can I say? I'm sorry. It was a stupid thing to do,
stupid and unforgiveable.
Forgive me?
It didn't mean anything, it was. . . .
It was nothing. I don't know why I did it. Anyway I'm
sorry.
Yes?
What else can I do?
Look, it's over now. It's done. I can't undo it. Can I?
What do you want, what do you want to happen now?
I've said I'm sorry, what else can I say? I'm sorry. It
won't happen again. I'm sorry.
Why don't you say something?
I've been hurt too, you know. You've done things to
hurt me.
Cruel things, not just thoughtless. Cruel. On purpose.
Do you think I've forgotten? To hurt me, to get your
own back. Well then. Can't you forget it?
Why shouldn't I then? Do what you've done? Do you
blame me?
Do you expect it all to be one-sided?
Do you blame me for wanting to get my own back?
Do you know what it's been like, living with you?
Do you know what I've been through?
Oh, God.
Oh, God, I hate you.
Oh, God, you bore me.

W	Well
	Goodbye
M	Oh
	You're going
W	Yes
	It's been
M	Yes
W	Well
M	It's been
W	Erm
	Thank you for
M	Yes
	Thank you
	Look, I don't
W	No
	It's all right
	No need to
M	Well anyway
	Thank you anyway and
W	Yes

Silence

M	You have an eyelash on your cheek.
W	Have I?
M	Just there.
W	Here?
M	There.
W	Is it gone?
M	No.
	There. It's gone.
	So.
W	I hope you don't
M	No
	It's been
	We've
W	It's
M	I
W	I
M	I

She cries

W   I

M   I

W   I

M   I

Silence, except that she cries

M   There was a blind man used to live nearby. I often saw
him leaving the house for his morning walk. He used to
have his wife with him. A woman, anyway, I assume it
was his wife. There was something pleasant about them,
an easiness in their behaviour, the way she let him
negotiate the gate, the way she held his arm, the way
they talked. I was always pleased to come across them.
Once or twice they came out of their gate ahead of me
and I followed them down the road. They talked
constantly, casually, in low voices, I could never catch
any of it. She looked at him while she talked, but he
looked ahead, I mean he kept his eyes—what does one
say?—he kept his face toward the front. They walked
slowly, but from the back, from the way they walked
and the way she held his arm it was difficult to tell that
she was leading him. She could have been an invalid,
walking slowly helped by him. Perhaps she was. In his
other hand he had his white stick which he used to find
the trees on his side, he was always on the outside of the
pavement. If I met them I'd quietly step out of the way,
onto the road; she never seemed to notice me and I
could never tell whether he heard me pass or not. Once
as they came toward me talking as usual, I glanced at
her and noticed that she'd closed her eyes too. I was
away for some time. I saw him again not long after I
got back. He was alone. He was holding a kind of
machine, a sort of echo-sounding device, I think, which
he waved about as he walked. It seemed to work quite
well. As we drew near each other I thought I might stop
and speak to him. I wanted to ask him how the thing
worked, how satisfactory it was. I'd have had to say: I
live just along the street, we've passed each other many
times only you don't know, or do you? How are you
getting along with your new machine? I didn't, though.
I thought he might ignore me, I might not speak loud
enough, he might just walk on and not even notice me. I

stepped into the road as usual. As he passed he said
thank you; without turning his head. I didn't answer.
I decided to say good morning next time we met, but I
haven't seen him since.
Then there was this woman used to walk up and down
the street — I used to see her quite a lot. I'd see her
through the window, or as I was leaving the house or
coming back, or cleaning the car. She was about — I
don't know; thirty — something, late thirties I suppose.
She'd walk up and down, stop suddenly, search the
ground, cross the road for no apparent reason. Now and
then she'd talk to herself, as if answering a question,
shaking her head. The first time I saw her I thought she
must be waiting for someone or looking for something
she'd dropped, and angry that they were late or that
she couldn't find it. She made me very uneasy. It was as
if she'd lost her cage; as if she'd lived her life in a cage
and woken up one day to find the bars had been taken
away. She was walking up and down looking for her
cage. She made me uneasy because there was something
so pent up I was afraid it might break out. I. . . . Well,
again, I considered the possibility of going up to her
and. She was standing on the other side of the street
one day looking at the ground, almost opposite the
house, and I considered the possibility of going up to
her and saying something. I don't think it was more
than an idea in my mind. I'd have had to say: Can I
help you in some way? I decided there were three
things she might have done: ignored me, or told me to
mind my own business, or screamed at me. But in any
case, I had my own troubles at that time. If I couldn't
do anything about my own — about people I was —
concerned with, I couldn't really. . . . It would have
been a kind of false luxury. Or something. Anyway.
She's gone now. They all go away eventually.
If only you were a stranger, we could perhaps do
something for each other.

     Touch
     Looking at each other, smiling
     Long pause

M   Hallo.
W   We met. Remember?

M   So we did. Yesterday, wasn't it?

W   What a good memory you have.

M   And the day before?

W   So we did. The day before as well.

M   And the day before that?

W   And the day before that and the day before that and the day before that.
How are you today?

M   I'm very well. How are you?

W   All the better for meeting you.

M   What are you laughing at?

W   You.

M   Me?

W   I'm laughing at meeting you again. It is very funny.
Every morning I wake up and there's this familiar
stranger waiting for me to meet him again.

M   How do you do?

W   How do you do?
What on earth are we laughing at?

M   Goodbye. It's been pleasant meeting you.

W   Goodbye. Won't it be.

              Exit

A Note on
"GAMES"

GAMES arose from a confrontation of four elements: myself;
a Reuter report; the company (of four) who were to perform the
piece, considered both as actors and as a particular group of
particular people; and the director of the group.

This script is not the final version, but the raw material from
which the actors, the director and I worked out a more or less
finished production.

There is therefore nothing definitive or sacrosanct about any
of the script. A different group performing the piece will
probably — I hope — want and need to sweat out their own
relationships to it, treating themselves as both actors (and
director) and individuals, so that the results of this process
become part of the production.

GAMES is about freedom, responsibility and choice, treated
not as theoretical concepts but as aspects of an actual event
which takes place during rehearsals and during each performance.
The play is about the fact of its being put on; but this fact
concerns not only the actors who have chosen to do it, but the
audience — which is both an audience and a collection of
individuals — who choose to accept it or reject it, to let it proceed
smoothly or to interrupt it or to wreck it. But it is not enough
to present an audience with the fact of a choice; the possibility
of using it must be put within their limits. Gauging these limits so
as to try to avoid the two extremes of frozen acceptance or an
untheatrical chaos means that there is no such thing as a
definitive performance.

James Saunders

PART I

2	Asked
3	Because
4	Where
1	The
2	They
3	Were
4	Yes
1	The
2	Yes
3	Mr
4	They
1	He
2	Maybe
3	Maybe
4	Reuter

Pause

1	Fort Benning
2	Former Private
3	Mr Meadlo
4	He declared
1	Mr Meadlo
2	Asked by
3	Because they
4	Where were
1	The prosecutor
2	They was
3	Were you
4	Yes I
1	The babies?
2	Yes.

Pause

3	Mr Meadlo
4	They might
1	He shot

Pause

2	He said

3   Maybe they. Maybe they would
                Pause
        Maybe th-. . . .
4   Reuter.
                Pause
1   January 12th.
2   Testified today that
3   Said he was afraid
4   He was prepared therefore
1   Who is twenty-three said that
2   Asked by the prosecutor
3   Because they was
4   Where were the
1   Captain Daniel asked.
2   They was in their
3   Were you afraid they would
4   Yes I was.
                Pause
3   Mr. Meadlo snapped back.
4   Might have been loaded over with
1   Out of fear that they were
2   He said
3   Maybe they would have a
        Maybe they
4   Reuter.
3   Maybe they would explode.
                Pause
1   Fort Benning Georgia January 12th.
2   Former Private Paul Meadlo testified today that he——
3   Mr Meadlo giving evidence for the second day at the
        court-martial of Lieutenant William Calley said he was
        afraid the——
4   He declared he was prepared therefore to follow orders
        to——
1   Mr Meadlo who is twenty-three said that he and
        Lieutenant Calley——
2   Asked by the prosecutor why he——

3   Because they was——
4   Where were the babies?

       Pause

2   They was in their mothers' arms.

       Pause

3   Maybe they would explode maybe they would explode
       maybe they would explode.

       Pause

1   Fort Benning Georgia January 12th.

2   Former Private Paul Meadlo testified today that he shot
       babies in the arms of their mothers in South Vietnam
       because he considered them all his enemy.

3   Mr Meadlo giving evidence for the second day at the
       Court-martial of Lieutenant William Calley said he was
       afraid the babies would be booby-traps which their
       mothers would throw at him.

4   He declared he was prepared therefore to follow orders
       to shoot and kill all Vietnamese no matter what their
       ages in the village of My Lai on March 16th 1968.

       Pause

1   Mr Meadlo who is twenty-three said that he and
       Lieutenant Calley shot and killed 100 to 150
       civilians in the village.

2   Asked by the prosecutor why he shot the Vietnamese
       Mr Meadlo said.

3   Because they was Vietcong.

       Pause

4   Where were the babies?
1   The prosecutor Captain Daniel asked.
2   They was in their mothers' arms.
3   Were you afraid they would attack you.

       Pause

4   Yes I was.
1   The babies?
2   Yes.

       Pause

3   Mr Meadlo snapped back.
       Pause
4   They might have been loaded over with grenades or
       anything their mothers could put on them.
1   He shot babies rather than search them out of fear that
       they were booby-trapped.
2   He said.
3   Maybe they would have a booby-trap on them. Maybe
       they would explode.
       Pause
1   Fort Benning Georgia January 12th.
2   Former Private Paul Meadlo testified today that he shot
       babies in the arms of their mothers in South Vietnam
       because he considered them all his enemy.
3   Mr Meadlo giving evidence for the second day at the
       court-martial of Lieutenant William Calley said he was
       afraid the babies would be booby-traps which their
       mothers would throw at him.
4   He declared that he was prepared therefore to follow
       orders to shoot and kill all Vietnamese no matter what
       their ages in the village of My Lai on March 16th 1968.
1   Mr Meadlo who is twenty-three said that he and
       Lieutenant Calley shot and killed 100 to 150 civilians in
       the village.
2   Asked by the prosecutor why he shot the Vietnamese
       Mr Meadlo said
3   Because they was Vietcong.
4   Where were the babies?
1   The prosecutor Captain Daniel asked.
2   They was in their mothers' arms.
3   Were you afraid they would attack you?
4   Yes I was.
1   The babies?
2   Yes.
3   Mr Meadlo snapped back.
4   They might have been loaded over with grenades or
       anything their mothers could put on them.
1   He shot babies rather than search them out of fear they
       were booby-trapped.

2   He said
3   Maybe they would have a booby-trap on them. Maybe
        they would explode.
4   Reuter.

PART II

Yes.

Oh yes.

It's beautiful.

Really extraordinary.

It's strange it has a kind of a.

It's very compelling.

The slow unfolding, that's what's so good, the way it
slowly kind of unfolds itself.

Exactly.

The way it starts with a few isolated words, meaningless
words, and gradually kind of unfolds itself. Really
extraordinary. I mean.

And the subject is so incredible.

It's really true?

Oh yes, it's true.

It's absolutely true. It's a Reuter report, a straight Reuter
report.

I remember reading it. It's verbatim. I couldn't quite take
it in, it was almost comic.

Incredible.

One can't of course. One reads the most incredible
reports, news items, I used to collect them.

Really?

I kept them in a book, a kind of a scrap book.

Chronicle of the unbelievable.

Exactly.

I must have missed it.

Of course, one does, that's the point. After a while the
mind stops noticing.

The incredible becomes the norm.

Exactly. That's why it's so necessary to find new ways of.

Of expressing the inexpressible.

Well. Yes, or not so much of expressing, as of. . . .

Making meaningful.

Exactly. Of giving meaning to the meaningless. And so, you see, one begins with isolated words, meaningless phrases out of context, so that the mind has to kind of reach out to grasp it and then suddenly finds itself caught in the unbelievable reality of it.

It's unreal believability.

Precisely.

Incredible. So that one grasps its full force.

You know what it's like?

So that suddenly one really pushes the veil aside, the veil of language, and grasps what it really means.

The meaning past the language.

You know what it's like? It's like a kind of verbal coitus interruptus.

Exactly.

Precisely.

Incredible.

Quite beautiful. We must do it again.

PART III

C   I used to find theatre such an incredibly artificial thing. You know?

D   Oh, I know. I know. I mean most of it bears no relation. . . .

C   I mean it bears no relation to what's actually happening —outside or —inside.

D   That's so true.

C   Of course one's so dependent on one's director and directors can be so narrow. They don't understand, what the problem is, they think it's to do with the part one's playing whereas it's nothing to do with the part it's to do with the whole conception of . . . I mean the whole value of what one's doing. You know?

D   Trivial plays. . . .

C   Well no, not only that. I mean one has to act in isolation from – life. I mean one only has to read the papers and one's assaulted by all the terrible things that are going on. My God, one thinks, what can I do, what should I do as a responsible human being? How can I record my protest, how can I do anything about it, anything? Then one goes to the theatre and one's supposed to forget. Leave it all outside. Isolate oneself from reality.

D   That's very true.

C   People are dying and suffering and the most terrible things are happening and. . . .

D   It's the same with one's private life.

C   Exactly. One happens to feel angry about something, one goes to the theatre feeling angry. "No darling" says the director, "You mustn't play it angry." "But I feel angry, I am angry." "That's your problem darling. Here you're an actress, just play the part." I mean. . . .

D   Exactly.

C   So one cuts oneself off from reality. One puts on the part, one gets into the part. What does it mean? Theatre becomes a kind of a refuge, a safe box, you know? where one never has to be oneself, one never has to feel anything, not really, not in one's head, one's heart, one's guts. . . . One becomes conditioned, brainwashed. One's told, keep that. Keep that. One learns to do nothing but pretend to recreate what has become stale and what was never real in the first place. One learns to keep oneself out.

D   Exactly.

C   Exactly. I don't want that. I want reality, not play-acting. Reality.

D   To be concerned.

C   It's so marvellous to be in a company where one is allowed to show concern.

D   To be oneself.

C   To be oneself, exactly. A responsible member of the community.

D   Feeling one's doing something.

C   Or at least that one's making the right noises.

D   It's so pleasant to be able to show one's on the right side.

PART IV

B   Mr Meadlo, can you make any assessment of the number of civilians you and Lieutenant Calley shot in the village?

A   I should say 100 to 150 sir.

B   Why did you shoot them?

A   Because they was Vietcong.

B   Where was the babies?

A   They was in their mothers' arms.

B   Were you afraid they would attack you?

A   Yes, I was.

B   The babies?

A   Yes. They might have been loaded over with grenades or anything their mothers could put on them.

B   So why did you not search them?

A   Out of fear that they were booby-trapped. Maybe they would have a booby-trap on them. Maybe they would explode.

B   Right.

A   I'm not very happy about "Out of fear that they were booby-trapped."

B   Why not?

A   It sounds a bit literary. Out of fear that.

B   Well what about, erm. . . .

C   For fear that?

B   No. I was afraid they might?

A   I was afraid they might — be booby-trapped. Maybe they would have a booby-trap on them, maybe they would explode. How does it sound?

B   So why did you not search them?

A   I was afraid they might be booby-trapped, maybe they would have a booby-trap on them, maybe they would explode.

B	Yes.
A	You don't think the repetition in that line is a little too much?
D	Oh don't change that line now, I think it's lovely. It sounds right.
B	No I like it. It gives that feeling of erm . . . a man with a limited vocabulary, you know? A simple man, only capable of these terribly simple thoughts which he sticks together one after another. Like a children's book, you know? Here is Dick with his dog. His dog's name is Fluff. I was afraid they might be booby-trapped. Maybe they would have a booby-trap on them. Maybe they would explode. It's absolutely right.
A	Fine, fine. . . .
D	Couldn't you try it like that? I mean do it very simply like a child.
B	What for?
D	I just thought it might be moving.
B	What, with a lisp?
D	It was only a suggestion. . . .
B	No, listen, try it . . . erm. . . . Try to separate the thoughts, he's working it out as he goes along, he's never stopped to ask himself why he did it and now suddenly, he's in the witness-box and for the first time he has to account for his actions. He's practically illiterate and he's suddenly having to explain. Yes?
C	Was he?
B	What?
C	Illiterate.
B	I said practically illiterate. I think we can assume that.
D	But in any case he would have gone over it all with his counsel, surely, so it's not really true that. . . .
B	Look can we just get on? Just think each line out, that's all I mean. Every thought is a kind of a hard won discovery. Maybe they would have a booby-trap on them. . . . Maybe they would explode. . . .
A	I was afraid they might be booby-trapped. . . . Maybe they would have a booby-trap on them. . . . Maybe they would explode!
	Pause

B   Well let's run through it again. Erm. . . . Oh, one
other thing. I don't really see this kind of man in this
kind of situation as the kind of man in the kind of
situation where he'd be looking at his questioner.

A   Why not?

B   I just don't think he would. Of course it's up to you.

A   You mean he's ashamed? Hangdog?

B   No, no, not hangdog. There's the snapped back bit,
where it says he snaps back. He wouldn't snap back if
he was hangdog.

A   That's what I thought. That's why I saw him as —
brazen.

B   Brazen?

A   Defiant, after all he had his orders, he was just obeying
orders, he says that, there's no reason not to think he's
in the right.

B   Oh, I don't see him like that at *all*.

A   No?

B   No no. Whether he was in the right or not is beside the
point.

A   To him, you mean?

B   Yes. Look, put yourself in his shoes. Here was this
simple illiterate in the jungle with his buddies, taking
orders, doing what he was told, fine, he was in the right.
But *now*, he's not in the jungle he's in Court, he's not
with his buddies any more he's in an alien environment,
surrounded by the very same kind of people he's always
taken orders from, but *now* they seem to be saying he
shouldn't have obeyed the orders in the first place. He's
confused, you see? Think of him as a — what? An animal,
a creature who's been taught to do a certain trick and
now is being threatened with punishment for doing the
same trick. By the same master! You see? He's confused,
he's — resentful if you like, because he doesn't
under*stand*.

A   So why doesn't he look at anyone?

B   Because he. . . .
Maybe you're right. It's up to you.

A   So shall I look at you or . . . ?

B	It just seemed dramatically right to me that he'd keep his eyes down, like a—what? Like a. . . . Until suddenly you get that marvellous moment where I say . . . erm. . . . Were you afraid they would attack you?
A	Yes I was.
B	The babies?
A	Yes. . . .
B	Mr Meadlo snapped back! Yes! And *that's* where he lifts his eyes and looks straight at his accuser. *Yes*, I did it, *yes*, I was afraid they might throw their babies at me, loaded with high explosives, are you trying to blame me, you are the ones to be blamed, you're the officers, you're my superiors and always have been, you made me what I am so that I could do your dirty work for you and enjoy it. Very well. I'm on your ground, I'm illiterate and confused and you're the educated ones, yes I shot the babies but somewhere still I have a little spark of self-respect, dignity, nobility even. Yes! Yes, you bastards! Yes?
A	Hm. . . .
C	Oh shit. . . .
B	What?
C	Sorry. Nothing. Do go on.
B	Right, shall we take it from the top again?

PART V

A	No you see, I'll tell you my dilemma. A, I'm an actor, right? Now what does this mean?
B	Could we just get on, do you think?
C	No, let him have his say.
D	Go on love.
C	Tell us about your dilemma.
A	It means I'm in a privileged position. It means I have the eye and ear of the public.
B	Not to say the nose and throat.
D	Let him have his say.

C   Take no notice, love, you go on about your dilemma.
        You've got the eye and nose of the public.

A   Look at the situation. Here's an actor on a stage, and
        there's a captive audience. Right? They've paid good
        money to sit in rows in a brick box. What for? For the
        privilege of listening to me talk. No, not to me. I'm an
        actor. I earn my living saying words for people who
        haven't got whatever it takes to do it themselves. I'm a
        sackful of other people's words. I mean sod the sack,
        it's the words they want. So they can be amused or
        moved or whatever it is they're after. That's Art. It's
        like throwing birdseed to fucking chickens. Here, chick
        chick chick, come and get your words, chick chick.

B   Insulting the audience will get you nowhere.

D   Shut up. Go on, love, we're all listening.

A   But B, I'm an individual, I'm a person.

C   What was A?

A   Actor, A I'm an actor.

B   A is for actor, up on a stage, B is for bullshit. . . .

D   Take no notice, love, you're doing marvellously.

A   I'm a member of my society. I'm Andy Norton for
        Christ sake. I've got my own views. I've got a feeling of
        responsibility to the society I live in. I've got this
        idea. . . . I believe that every time. . . .

B   *(sings)* "I believe that every time a flower grows . . . "

A   I believe it's everyone's duty to say what they think
        about their society! Whenever they're in a position to!
        I'm a democrat, I don't believe in silent majorities,
        right?

C   Right love.

D   Right.

A   Right. So what have we got?

C   What?

D   AB.

B   A plus B.

A   What we've got is me. Andy Norton. On a stage by
        himself. A captive audience waiting for words. Fuck the
        play, there's more important things. I'm not . . . I don't
        have to follow the script. I'm a free man on a stage with

an audience, I can say what I like and you can't switch
me off, you've got to listen to what I've got to say,
listen or stop me or fuck off. If I think the world we're
making for ourselves is a load of shit I can say so and I
can tell you why! I. . . . Oh fucking hell. . . .

D   What's the matter love?

A   Don't you see? That's it, that's my dilemma. What am I
doing? Standing here talking a lot of meaningless—
bloody. . . . It's the stage, it turns us all into buffoons.
Why, what happens? I'm real, I swear it. Offstage I'm
real. I get onstage and suddenly I don't believe a word
I'm saying! Who'd guess I'm a dedicated acid freak, hands
up who'd guess. Oh, it's pathetic. Theatre turns us all
into idiots. . . .

C   There there, give him a handkerchief.

D   Poor love.

B   The cunt.

A   Go on, laugh, laugh. I'm not funny, I'm a person! No
I'm not. I'm on a stage, I'm an actor. I'm pretending,
I'm *acting* real. What's the difference? Even when you're
real you're only real because you're pretending to be
real. Look at me, pretending to give a shit what a
performance.

B   Blub blub.

A   Fuck it, I've had enough. I've had enough of pretending
to be other people. I've had enough of pretending to be
myself. I want to *be* myself!

                Cry for a moment.

Down with consumer society! An end to the Imperialist
wars! Decency and dignity for all! Oh, it's no good.

                Cry. Pause

B   Yes, that wasn't bad. I think we could cut it a bit.

A   Do you think so?

C   I found it quite funny. Did you find it funny?

D   Yes, I thought it was quite funny. And a teeny bit
moving, you know. At the end.

C   Yes, a teeny bit.

B   You know you cut a line, do you?

A   Did I?

B   My favourite bit. The bit about, erm, it isn't the
        satisfied ones who are guilty. . . .
A   Where is the guilt in Society? Not with the satisfied, not
        with the content —
A   —they are the innocents. We are the guilty; the
B   dissatisfied, the sick at heart. If society is to change it
        must be through us. Is it enough, will history accept
        that it was enough, that I stood on a stage and acted
        out my concern.
B   Mm. . . .
A   I like that bit.
                        Pause
C   Are you really an acid head?
A   Yes.
C   Then why *don't* you?
A   What?
C   Do something.
A   What on stage?
C   Yes.
A   But it wouldn't be fair, would it? I mean rocking the
        boat. Wouldn't be fair to one's fellow actors. One has to
        obey the rules.
B   Exactly.
D   And anyway, no one would listen.
B   Good. That's good. A bit more fire in that: "Anyway no
        one would listen." And anyway, no one would listen!
D   And anyway, no one would listen!
B   Lovely, darling. Keep that.

PART VI

C. with book, reading in

C   Why did you shoot them?
A   Because they was Vietcong.
B   Yes, now, could you put some venom into that
        Veetcong? Oh, by the way, Veetcong, I think, not
        Vietcong. Venom. It's a taboo word, not a taboo word,

a . . . what's the word? I mean, it's the most emotive word you know, it stands for everything you've been conditioned to think of as the ultimate, erm, evil. Veetcong. This is your justification, this word, it's all there. Yes?

A   Because they was Veetcong. Because they was Veetcong.

B   Better. Right, from the top again.

C   Mr Meadlo, how many civilians did you and Lieutenant Calley kill?

Pause

D   100 – 150.

A   I know. I was recollecting.

B   Wait a minute.
Yes I think you ought to have that answer pat. Straight off. You've worked it all out with your counsel.

D   But you said. . . .

B   From the top.

C   Mr Meadlo, how many civilians did you and Lieutenant Calley kill?

A   100 – 150, sir.

B   That's good. I like that touch of sarcasm on the sir. Go on.

C   Why did you shoot them?

A   Because they was Vietcong.

C   Where were the babies?

A   They was in their mothers' arms.
I thought that had to be really matter of fact. Do you think?

B   Acting against the line, you mean?

A   Well it's all there isn't it? I mean, babies in their mothers arms, it's a kind of schmaltz thing. . . .

D   Kitsch.

C   Babies in their mothers' arms. A kitsch thing.

A   Schmaltz.

B   Yes. . . . Yes, I think you're right. Corney.

D   Schmaltz.

A   Kitsch.

C   Babies in their mothers' arms. Schmitz.

D   Kaltch.

C   I mean it's really been overdone, right. Babies in their
         mothers arms.

A   Babies in their. . . . Real Schmaltz. . . .

PART VII

B   Let's get our thinking straight on this. A theatre is a
         theatre. It's not a pulpit. It's not a political platform.
         It's not a Court of Justice, and it's not, God forbid, the
         inside of anybody's mind. Not yours, not hers, not hers,
         not mine, not anyone's. Your mind is your own affair;
         your conscience is your own affair, your political or
         social or metabloodiphysical views are your own affair
         and whether you wet your bed at night is your own
         affair. We don't want to know, nobody wants to know.
         Your mind belongs inside your head. We are not inside
         somebody's head, we are on a stage, we are actors, we
         are doing theatre, in other words we are pretending, we
         are choosing to pretend, we are presenting the
         rehearsed and refined results of a series of pretences in
         order to entertain an audience. If you want to be real,
         fuck off, you're in the wrong business.

         Having said that, having defined our activity as that of
         the buffoon, the next question is: must we be *only* that?
         Is it possible to use theatre in two contradictory ways:
         as an end in itself, as a box within which we choose to
         forget or ignore the outside world while we amuse
         ourselves and each other; and also as a *means*, as a
         means towards an end which has something to do with
         the improvement of the society we live in? I think it is
         possible. How? I'll tell you. The link is choice. Choice.
         Choice is our business. By choosing to be buffoons, we
         entertain. But by showing the audience that we have
         chosen this role, that we are constantly at every
         moment choosing this role anew, by showing the
         audience that we have not retreated into an apologetic
         and fatalistic acceptance of our role but have merely
         accepted it for the moment in a conscious decision
         which we renew at every moment – by doing this it's

possible, just possible, that something might start to
happen. Look we're all optimists. We all believe in the
improvability of Society by a voluntary, democratic
process. So why doesn't it? What goes wrong? Why does
a man, an ordinary law-abiding man, go out under
orders to a foreign country and kill a baby?
Why?
I'll tell you why: because he didn't know he didn't have
to. He'd never been told this simple fact, never
perhaps in his life, the simple fact that he is his own man.
That it isn't enough to follow the pattern, to be defined
from the outside, to obey orders, to accept other
people's images. That you can't be *given* freedom. That
we are all our own men. That a man is as real as he is
vulnerable. That a man is as real as he rejects other
people's images. That he is as real as he chooses—to be.
That it's both necessary and entertaining to put oneself
at constant risk, in constant danger, by constantly
questioning one's acceptances.
That's what we can deal with. That's our currency. What
we can show is a group of people who have chosen to
make ourselves vulnerable, to put ourselves in danger, to
act without precedent, to take the chance, to choose, to
be free; and who enjoy doing it.

> *Pause. Applause from the others*
> *Pause*

D   You hypocritical shit.

B   What?

D   You arrogant bastard. You really have it all worked out,
don't you? Look at us, choosing to be free to help
Society. Big fucking deal. How nice to be right, how
pleasant to know one's motives. So that we can carry on
choosing to be free to choose to act which is what we
wanted to do in the first place, while the world goes
rotten all round us. But we don't bother about that,
outside there's a war on but all we have to do is show
everyone else what to do about it. Teaching people to
choose, big deal. We know how to choose already of
course, and what do we choose to do? We talk about
theatre. Outside there's a war going and we talk about
theatre. You hypocritical arrogant bastard. If we can't
do anything about it why the hell expect them to?

Pause

A   I think she's right. I don't really think you can justify. . . .

B   I'm not trying to justify anything.

C   It sounded like it to me.

A   Of course you were.

B   Look all I was saying was that possibly we might be able in some way to. . . .

A   Yes I know, to help Society.

B   Don't you think we do any good then? You think we're absolutely bloody useless.

A   From that point of view, yes. I should think so.

B   Then what are you doing here? What are you doing with this useless outfit? You're always on about the state of society, why waste time here, why aren't you at the barricades?

A   You want to know why, I'll tell you. Because I'm a coward.

B   Oh very. . . .

A   Because I can't stand the sight of blood, that's why I'm here. Because I'm a bloody squeamish yellowbelly! What's your excuse.

B   Very convenient!

A   It's not as a matter of fact, it's a bit disgusting and I'm ashamed of it. But at least I'm honest about it. What about you? What about Mr Social Bigmouth? What the fuck are you doing here? Prating about Society and risk and danger, you make me puke!

B   There are other ways of changing Society than —

A   There are no other ways of changing Society than with a bloody gun! Get that into your thick skull. 1971 in the Western Hemisphere is a year or two late for your nice — civilized notions of poncing about on stage to help the what was it, the voluntary democratic processes! Shit to democratic processes! You're doing something or you're a coward or you're a reactionary bastard, you're with it or you're against it! Just don't make excuses. Why did you shoot them?

B   Because they was Vietcong!

A   The babies?

B   They was in their mothers' bloody arms!
                    Fight. After a while, stop
                    Kiss. Applause from others
A   That was very good.
B   Once more from the top.

PART VIII

We are only actors.

Pretenders.

We don't pretend to be God.

We're confused.

That, really is all we have to say to you.

We are completely confused.

We had some beautiful discussion on the way, taking in
private responsibility, public responsibility, collective
guilt, the necessity for and the futility of direct action,
the need for revolutionary change as distinct from
evolutionary progress and the need for evolutionary
progress as distinct from revolutionary change.

On humility and arrogance.

On the actor as puppet.

On the audience as puppet.

On everyone as puppet.

On what it is to pretend to pretend to pretend to pretend
—to pretend.

On choosing to choose and choosing not to, now there's
a paradox for you.

It went round in an almost complete circle. What
remained was the following. I think.

We are not God. We are confused. We do what we do
because we do what we do. We don't like—certain
things—that happen from time to time. And don't
know how to stop them happening.

And feel guilty about that.

And find it's quite pleasant to feel guilty.

It makes for a very good argument.

And wish we had more humility.

And know that if faced with a few pertinent questions by our great grandchildren, what did you do in the . . . , great-grand-daddy? We should be stuck for an answer.

Assuming we have great grandchildren.

In any case, we shan't be there. But it makes for a very good discussion.

Printed by The Kingfisher Press, London NW10 7AS

Lightning Source UK Ltd.
Milton Keynes UK
UKOW05f1815011116
286649UK00025B/604/P